Black Cats, Hoot Owls, and Water Witches

Black Cats, Hoot Owls, and Water Witches
Beliefs, Superstitions, and Sayings from Texas

edited by

Kenneth W. Davis & Everett Gillis

University of North Texas Press, Denton

Requests for permission to reproduce material from this work
should be sent to the
University of North Texas Press, P. O. Box 13856, Denton, Texas 76203-3856

LIBRARY OF CONGRESS CATALOGING-IN-PUBLICATION DATA

Black cats, hoot owls, and water witches : beliefs, superstitions, and sayings
from Texas / edited by Kenneth W. Davis and Everett A. Gillis.
      p. cm.
   ISBN 0-929398-06-8
      1. Folklore—Texas. 2. Superstition—Texas. 3. Texas—Social life
and customs. I. Davis, Kenneth W., 1932—   . II. Gillis, Everett, 1914—
1989.
GR110.T5B54 1989
398' .09764—dc   20   89-27779
                                                    CIP

For all the Paisanos in the

Texas Folklore Society

Contents

Illustrations

Introduction

Folklore concerns itself with everyday life as well as the world of myth. Long before daily around-the-clock weather reports became available, a West Texas housewife knew from hard-earned experience the truth of the West Texas saying: "It's bad luck to hang your clothes out on the line if there is a bank of blue haze in the west." The bad luck is, of course, what happens to freshly washed clothes still wet on the line when a dust storm hits. However, once a saying is embedded in an oral tradition, no one expects or requires specific proof to support it—no more than in the case of the elderly farmer in Robert Frost's poem "Mending Wall," who, pressed by the speaker in the poem for a reason why there should be a wall between their properties, offered only his father's saying: "Good fences make good neighbors."

Folklore is often told in vigorous, robust, and colorful language. We delight to hear a bit of folk-say phrased both neatly and laconically: "I am as hungry as a bitch wolf with puppies"; or, "My mouth is so dry I am spitting cotton."

Ideally, folklore lives in the minds and hearts of a people; those who create it sustain it. However, to print folklore helps to ensure its survival. The folklore we present here varies. We include superstitions and sayings, weather lore, and traditional observations on animal and human life. Also included are remedies and cures, as well as proverbial wit and wisdom.

Folk sayings may vary distinctly from one region to the next, making collecting regional sayings, such as these from Texas, vital. We hope our readers have as much fun browsing through this book as we did preparing it.

E. A. G. and K. W. D.
Texas Tech University
Lubbock, Texas

Field and Farm

Moon and Stars

If you go to sleep with the moon shining in your face, you
will go crazy.

Judy Moffett, Lubbock

You will have bad luck if you look at the moon through trees
or bushes.

Barbara Holloway, Dallas

See a falling or shooting star, make a wish; it will come
true.

Martha Kissinger, Fort Worth

If there is a ring around the moon, count the number of
stars within that ring. Then you will know how
many days there are before there will be rain.

Edward Perkins, Holland

Star light, star bright,
First star I see tonight,
Wish I may, wish I might,
Have this wish I wish tonight.

Martha Kissinger, Fort Worth

The position of the moon predicts weather; if it is turned so
that water will run out of it, there will be rain; if it
is turned so that it will hold water, there will be no
rain.

Grace Hogan, Wichita Falls

At the first glimpse of the new moon, make a wish over your
left shoulder and don't look back.

Vester Yeary, Cameron

If a falling star falls from west to east, dry weather is in
store; if a star falls from east to west, expect plenty
of rain.

Glen Randal, Gatesville

Expect changes of the weather when the moon changes.

Porter Robertson, Posey

If a child is born when the Evening Star is at its brightest,
that child is blessed forever.

Lucy Mannering, Jacksboro

If you can see the Big Dipper in February, you can predict
the coming spring season. If the Dipper holds water,
the spring will be a wet one; if it won't hold water,
there won't be enough rain to bother with planting
crops.

Sharon McCreary, Lubbock

The farmer who sees the Morning Star three times in a row
is sure to have a good crop.

Tate Branscomb, Lometa

Beware if you see the stars in the daytime before dusk.

Joe Wilson, Robstown

If you wish on a star, don't tell anybody or your wish won't
come true.

Clarice Fundel, Bridgeport

It is always good luck to make a wish under a new moon.

Mrs. Frank Bluemel, San Antonio

Animals are always restless on moonlit nights.

Mrs. W. O. Schafroth, Harlingen

Look at a new moon, throw salt over your left shoulder, and
your wishes will come true.

Doris Pippin, San Antonio

Butcher the hogs in the light of the moon if you want
lots of grease.

Herbert R. Rawlings, Belton

Weather Wisdom

Unusually fat dove and quail mean the coming of a severe winter.

Paula Steele, Dallas

If the sun is shining when you are born, you will have a happy life.

Phyllis Sparks, Idalou

The weather in Texas shows that God has a sense of humor.

Millie Smith, Munday

Heavy corn crop, hard winter; one extreme season follows another.

Dorothy Colfee, Lubbock

When flies swarm on the screens, it is a sure sign of rain.

George Wilson, Lubbock

If Christmas Eve is a moonlit night, the next year will not
be a good crop year.

O. V. Warren, De Leon

If the sun sets behind a bank of clouds on Sunday, it is sure
to rain before the following Wednesday.

Sue Housely, Lubbock

Three months from the first thunder in September, there
will be snow.

L. C. Alcorn, Odessa

If the wind blows strongly for three days from the east, all
the devils in Hell can't keep it from raining.

Emma Dodds, San Antonio

If it rains on the 14th day of July, it will rain for 40 days.
If it does not rain on that day, it will not rain for 40
days.

H. M. Gathling, San Antonio

When the thunder is heard in February, all the unhatched
babies of a setting goose will die in the shell.

Darleen Stevens, Lubbock

If water rises to the surface of a dry creek bed, it is a sign
of rain.

Diana Stafford, Lubbock

Moss coming to the top of the water is a sign of rain.

Mrs. A. Vick, Caddo

If it is raining and the sun is shining at the same time, the
devil is beating his wife and it will rain at the same
time tomorrow.

David Hurt, Lubbock

Thunder means that God has turned over his apple barrel.

Deane Smith, Bryan

When the mesquite blooms in the spring, there will be no
more killing frosts.

Bertha Shauver, Lubbock

A red sunset signifies the coming of hail.

Tulisha Shahan, Bracketville

For every foggy day in February, it will rain on the same
day in June.

Frank Medley, Lubbock

The morning red and the evening gray
Will set the traveller on his way;
But the morning gray and the evening red
Will bring down rain on the traveller's head.
Ernest Rudd, New Home

When the prairie dogs bank dirt up around their den
entrances, watch for a gully washer.
Sammie Miller, Brownfield

If it thunders before seven, it will rain before eleven.
Sylvia Poovey, Hale Center

If chickens run for cover when a rain comes up, the rain
won't last long, but if the chickens stay out in the
rain, you can expect rain all day. The chickens
know that if the rain is going to be a short one,
there is no point in getting wet, but if the rain is
going to last all day, they must be out in it to search
for food.
Mrs. C. P. Davis, Lubbock

A person's corns will hurt before a rain comes up.
Elizabeth Hawkins, Lubbock

If it rains on Easter Sunday, it will rain on seven consecutive Sundays.

> *R. A. Bain, Amarillo*

The morning rain is like an old woman's dance; it is soon over.

> *Judy Campbell, Fort Worth*

If it thunders on the first day of February, it will be a wet spring.

> *Martha Kissinger, Fort Worth*

If the sun goes down behind a cloud, it will rain the next day.

> *Martha Kissinger, Fort Worth*

It will rain 31 days after the first fog in February.

> *James Hogan, Lubbock*

If the cattle on the range drift against the fence in a closely packed bunch, there will be a blue norther.

> *Willie Haithcock, Plainview*

A wind from the east brings rain.

> *Eleanor Cossiart, San Antonio*

If there is a halo around the sun, it will rain soon.

Marshall Hayes, Lott

Crow on the fence,
Rain will go hence,
Crow on the ground,
Rain will come down.

Ernest Rudd, New Home

If it rains on Monday, it will rain three days of that week.

Mattie Green, Lubbock

Fish bite better during a rain.

Martha Kissinger, Fort Worth

Big drops mean little rain.

Clarice Doughitt, Lubbock

A wind blowing from the south for three days means rain
   is on the way.

Mrs. A. Vick, Caddo

A cloud won't come up against the moon.

Jack Eubank, Waco

If the smoke from the ginstack goes down, it is a sign of
    rain.

Mattie Green, Lubbock

Frost on a moonlit night won't kill.

Pat Guess, Bay City

If it thunders within the first ten days of January, it will
    frost in April.

Mrs. M. B. Guess, Bay City

When tarantulas come out, it is a sign of rain.

D. Burns, Guthrie

Smoke settling to the ground is a sure sign of falling
    weather.

Willie Haithcock, Plainview

If the west is red on Sunday evening, it will rain before
    Wednesday.

Marie Hill, Lubbock

Thick shucks on corn means a cold winter ahead.

Claude Davis, Lubbock

Thunder will cause milk to sour.

Marie Hill, Lubbock

The first killing frost of the year will occur two months
after the date of the first north winds to blow for
three days in August.

Mildred Hoghland, Perryton

It will rain somewhere within sight every day in June if it
rains on June first.

David Hurt, Lubbock

If you see a sundog (a kind of partial rainbow near the sun)
before noon, there will soon be rain.

B. F. Kellum, Lubbock

If late in the evening,
The horses and cows are frisky at play,
It surely will rain the very next day.

Cecil Slover, Lubbock

It will frost forty days after the first norther in the fall.

W. D. Swickheimer, Beaumont

You can expect a rain when a slack rope tightens.

Kay Lanceley, Big Spring

In the fall or winter, if cattle become restless or begin to
    drift, it is a sign of bad weather.
Criss Moody, Crowell

See a rainbow before 8:00, you will have rain before 11:00.
Marie Hill, Lubbock

The cooing of the rain-crow is a sure sign of rain.
Claudette McInnis, May

A red sunset means the sand will blow tomorrow.
Mrs. C. P. Davis, Lubbock

When a turtle is going west with his head out and uphill,
    it is going to rain.
Jeanette Moody, Crowell

Hot and cold puffs of wind when there are greenish clouds
    in the sky indicate a good possibility for hail.
Mrs. Laura Perkins, Bartlett

When a blue bank of haze appears on the northern horizon,
    a blue norther is coming in. In West Texas, the
    same sort of haze in the northwest skies in spring is
    a sign of a coming duststorm. Women who are
    weatherwise won't hang their clothes out on a line
    on such a day.
Ernest Sigmon, Amarillo

More than thirteen blackbirds on a fence with their tails to
the north is a sure sign of a coming blue norther.
Ernest Rudd, New Home

Whirlwinds going uphill are sure signs of dry weather.
Mrs. Alma Taylor, Wellman

If you can get in the exact center of a whirlwind as tall as
your house, you will see the devil.
Stella Davis, Granger

Sheet lightning is a sign of wind.
Mildred Shelton, Borger

When a pregnant sow runs around with a stick in her
mouth, there will be a blue norther. A granny lady
knows why this is true: the pregnant sow with the
stick is building a nest to protect her babies from the
cold.
Mrs. C. P. Davis, Lubbock

Because heat expands all bodies, the days in summer are
longer than those in winter.
Rex Ellis, Dallas

A cold spree in the late spring is blackberry winter.
Mrs. Alma Taylor, Wellman

Onion skin very thin,
Milk winter coming in;
Onion skin thick and tough,
Coming winter cold and rough.

Loretta Spinner, Lubbock

Three consecutive fogs in August mean frost sixty days
later.

Margaret Phelps, Beaumont

Jackrabbits running and playing around noon time is a
sign of a change in the weather.

Bobbie Warren, De Leon

If a cow kicks her hind feet straight out behind her, it will
rain within three days. And if a mule jumps in the
air and clicks his hooves together, there will be a day
of rain for each time his hooves click.

O. V. Warren, De Leon

When dry land terrapins are crawling uphill, it is sure to
rain, but if they are crawling downhill, the rain is
over and it will be dry.

O. V. Warren, De Leon

If ants remain in the ground all day, it will rain.

Kay Lanceley, Big Spring

Water Witching

If you have the gift to witch for water, you must never
charge anyone for witching him a well. If you charge
for witching a well, you will lose the gift.
Claude P. Davis, Lubbock

Some water witches tie a little bottle of water from a
nearby spring to the end of a peach limb. Where the
limb turns down, there is water.
Gladys Cage, San Antonio

Use a green witch (a Y-shaped branch from a tree or bush).
If it pulls down, water is there. Put a four-bit piece
in your hand and if it does not pull down, the water
is salty. If it pulls down, the water is all right.
Gladys Cage, San Antonio

To determine the depth of the water underground, take a
straight green stick which is limber and hold it still.
When it starts shaking, the number of shakes
indicates the number of feet down to water.
Marian Hath, San Antonio

If you do not begin digging a witched well within three
days after a witch has located it, you will lose the
water.

Michael Hardway, Plainview

You must never talk to a witch who is walking about
with his divining rod or tree branch; if you talk to
him, you will break the spell.

Lucy Devereaux, Davilla

A water witch will have his favorite type of tree from
which to get his 'witch.' Some witches prefer elm
branches; others insist that only a peach tree
provides an accurate 'witch' and still others swear
by willow branches.

Doris DiQuenzio, Hondo

There are a few witches who do not need branches from
trees; these selected few can tell by a feeling in
their elbows where water is. The people walk
over a field or pasture with their arms stretched
out in front of them.

Lonnie Dillard, Lubbock

A man who never saw his mother is likely to be able to witch
    wells.

> *Claude Davis, Lubbock*

Witch a well on a Sunday and you will lose the gift.

> *Grady Ferguson, Salado*

The gift for witching water wells is not passed down
    from father to son.

> *H. L. Perkins, Bartlett*

Planting and Growing

Crops, Flowers, and a Goat or Two

The best day to plant the spring garden is always Good
  Friday.

> *Kay Graham, Lubbock*

Some curious names for plants and the like:

Fireweed for willow herb.
Cow-lily for jimson weed.
Calico bush for mountain laurel.
Mexican moss for portulaca.
Thimblehead (a plant whose flower resembles a thimble
  with a fringe around the bottom).
Fire Wheel, or Indian Pink (a plant whose flower re-
  sembles a small, flaming wheel).
Buffalo clover (looks like a blue bonnet but makes cattle go
  crazy as bed bugs).

> *Ernest Sigmon, San Antonio*

If you want to have a good crop year for plants and animals,
  you must be absolutely sure that the first living
  creature that crosses your threshold on New Year's
  Day is male.

> *Eugenia McNeill, Crosbyton*

Things that grow under the ground such as carrots and
    potatoes should be planted when the sign is in the
    fishes.

Mrs. A. Vick, Caddo

To make a peach tree bear, tie a bottle or bottles to any limb
    with a string.

Gladys Cage, San Antonio

A short horse is quickly curried.

Mrs. Laura Perkins, Bartlett

To make peach, pear, or plum trees bear heavily, drive a
    few rusty nails into their trunks and paint a shirt of
    whitewash on each trunk.

Emmett Ware, Belton

Old timers in West Texas think that if the mesquite trees
    grow a big crop of beans, it is a sure sign of a coming
    dry year.

Mrs. L. R. Holder, Snyder

When Spanish goats come in from the pasture for salt from
    the salt block, this is a good time to plant a garden
    for a rain is on the way.

Joe Trejo, Salado

If you thank the person who gives you a plant, it will die.

Kay Lanceley, Big Spring

Plants that grow on top of the ground such as squash
and beans should be planted when the sign is in
the twins.

Virginia Adams, Lubbock

If you have eggs setting in February and it thunders, you
won't get a good hatch.

Eugenia McNeill, Crosbyton

Never, never put a hen to set on a Sunday.

Mrs. Laura Perkins, Bartlett

If you plant your garden on a Sunday, you will have to pay
the preacher or the devil.

Ben Hylin, Lampasas

Plants with eyes, such as potatoes, must never be planted
on the dark of the moon; they can't see to grow then.

Jerry Hays, Holland

To kill Johnson grass, plow it up three feet deep in the dark
of the moon in August.

Jim Cooper, Holland

Cotton won't grow for three years all around a patch of
ground which has been struck by lightning.

Alexander Wilson, Brownfield

Texas land is so poor it takes twenty years to rust a nail.

Jim Lee, Denton

Cotton blooms should be pollinated by wild honey bees and bumblebees. Such cotton plants produce a better grade of cotton.

Grady Ferguson, Salado

Hang old red flannel underwear on the fence next to the corn patch to keep varmints out. Having a mean dog helps, too.

Bessie Moxley, Temple

Keep beetles away from squash by spraying onion juice on the plants.

Robert Jackson, Lubbock

To keep coons and varmints out of the cornfield, don't plant the outside row.

Yantis Freed, Taylor

Texas land is so rich you can plant a crowbar at night and harvest tenpenny nails in the morning.

Barbara Thomas, Dallas

The grain-bearing plants must always be planted on the increase of the moon.

Franklin Persky, Rowena

If you can get a seventh son of a seventh son (or the seventh daughter) in any family to help you shell your corn, you will have a bumper crop.

Mrs. C. P. Davis, Lubbock

Red pepper fed to hens will make them lay many eggs if it
holds out long enough.

Willie Randal, Longview

If it rains on the longest day of the year, the 'mast' (pecans,
walnuts, berries, etc.) will fall.

Noah Young, Desdemona

At harvest's end, set aside some corn and grapes for a
friend.

Pearlene Jameson, Wichita Falls

Dehorn cattle when the signs of the zodiac are going down
into the legs. (This will prevent bleeding better than
if the dehorning is done when the signs are in the
head.)

O. L. Sutton, Matador

When the farmer's calf crop consists chiefly of heifer calves,
the farmer's crop will be good; but if the calves are
mainly bulls, he will have to sell the calves in order
to feed himself and his family.

O. V. Warren, De Leon

Worms, Frogs, Roosters,
Crickets, and Other Critters

If an inch worm crawls on you, he is measuring you for your
shroud.

> *Janice Gates, San Antonio*

If you find a measuring worm on you, you will get a new
dress, shirt, or trousers because the worm is
measuring you for the new garment.

> *Elsie Crow, San Antonio*

Whistling girls and crowing hens
Will always come to some bad end.

> *Mrs. Laura Perkins, Bartlett*

If a redbird crosses the road in front of you, you will have
visitors.

> *Alma Reed, Granger*

If a rooster crows toward the door, company is coming; if
the rooster crows with its head away from the door,
someone in the family is going to make a trip.

> *G. C. Nathanson, Brownsville*

If you run over a horned toad with a wagon wheel, your cow
will go dry.

> *R. D. Filler, Fort Worth*

If you play with a horned toad and make it mad, it will spit
    blood.

Jane Buchanan, Lubbock

Playing with toads will cause warts.

Anna Bridges, San Antonio

If a horned toad spits in one's eyes, the person will go blind.

Maude Barker, Gilliland

If you step on a cricket, there will be rain.

R. D. Filler, Fort Worth

It is bad luck to kill a cricket.

Ethel Harrell, San Antonio

The first mourning dove that you hear for the New Year
    will be in the direction of your next move.

Anne Bridges, Belton

If a black cat runs in front of you, make a cross over your
    chest and spit; this keeps bad luck from befalling
    you.

Mattie Green, Lubbock

If a cow is lost, hunt for a granddaddy longlegs spider and
    he will lift one leg, and that leg will point in the
    direction of the lost cow.

Lonnie Dillard, Lubbock

If you have lost a herd of cattle on open range, find a tumble
bug (dung beetle). His feelers will point in the
direction of the herd.

Lonnie Dillard, Lubbock

Killing a spider is bad luck. When you find a spider in the
house, get it on a broom or dust mop and shake it off
out of doors.

Elsie Crowe, San Antonio

To get a doodle bug to come out of his house, take a small
stick or your index finger and go round and round in
the doodle bug's hole and sing a tune:

Doodle bug, doodle bug,
Your house is on fire
And all your children will burn.
Doodle bug, doodle bug,
Fly away home.

John Coffey, Itasca

If you see a white horse, lick your thumb, stamp it into your
left hand and clap your hands. Keep your eyes
closed and make a wish. It will come true.

Marshall A. Hayes, Lott

If you find a ladybug, it is good luck. But if you kill or injure
the ladybug, it is bad luck.

Loretta Spinner, Lubbock

If you cut off the end of a puppy's tail and bury it under the
front doorstep, the puppy will never leave home.
O. W. Richardson, Lamesa

If you see the shadow of a raven without seeing the raven,
you will go somewhere you never expected to.
Lucy Shuffield, San Antonio

To be a successful pig-raiser, one must first steal a pig.
D. L. Shuffield, Lubbock

Goats and sheep always come to the house from far away
pastures to lick salt before there is to be a change in
the weather.
Claude Davis, Belton

A cat will cross three rivers in three days to return home
after it has been taken from home by its owners.
Lewis Vicknair, Belton

When a stray cat comes to live with you, it is a sign that a
baby is coming.
Mrs. Dove Hott, Dallas

To kill a cat is seven years bad luck.
Harold Hood, Fort Worth

A black snake will milk a cow dry.
Mrs. Laura Perkins, Bartlett

A male cat with four different colors in its fur is a priceless
   possession which will bring good luck and good
   harvests and lots of bull calves.

Sue Allen, San Antonio

When the wind is in the East,
Fish bite the least.

Nita Murray, Wilson

If a dirt-dauber wasp builds a nest outside your bedroom
   window, you can expect lots of company in the
   coming winter.

Lee Holland, Belton

Guinea hens will not lay their eggs until the blackberry
   bushes have bloomed.

Grady Ferguson, Salado

If you are going up a path and see where a snake has
   crossed, spit in the trail before you cross it and it
   will rain.

Phyllis Reed, Brownwood

A horse is worth $100 for every time he can roll over.

John Jones, Ozona

If a dragonfly lands on your fishing pole while you are
   fishing, you will catch a fish.

A. R. Woodall, Eureka

Some say a coyote turns to a ghost at night.
                              Eugenia McNeill, Crosbyton

If cattle are standing in the field, fish will be biting, but if
      the cattle are lying down, the fish will not bite.
                              Bob Hilton, Borger

If a white cat crosses your path, you will have good luck.
                              Mary Hillis, Seymore

It is bad luck to have a rabbit cross your path from right to
      left; but if the rabbit crosses from left to right, good
      luck will follow.
                              Lester Dudley, Lubbock

If a coyote comes near your door, trouble will strike your
      home.
                              Clarice Doughitt, Brownfield

If a dog is lying with his head facing out the front door, it
      means someone is coming into the family.
                              Earline Ince, Lubbock

In Central Texas, the armadillo is known as the poor man's
      pig.
                              Lonnie Wheeler, Lubbock

A rattlesnake will not die until sundown.
                              Jack Tomlinson, Amarillo

When your horse is snake bit, read three verses of
   Matthew, Chapter I, and call the horse's name after
   every sentence you read. This will cure the snake
   bite.

Joyce Sales, Lubbock

Snakes won't crawl over a rope on the ground. So, circle a
   rope around your bedroll before turning in.

Lonnie Dillard, Lubbock

When a black cat crosses in front, pull a thread from your
   dress and spit on it.

Liz Gillis, Lubbock

If you swallow a snake,
You will die of a bellyache.

Jeanette Martin, Bryan

It is bad luck to move a cat. If it moves, then leaves, it is
   bad luck. If it moves and stays, however, it is good
   luck.

Barbara Holloway, Dallas

People in river bottom areas plant gourd vines around
   their homes to keep snakes away. Likewise, castor
   beans will ward off mosquitoes.

George Wilson, Lubbock

If the first snake you see in the year is dead, you will have
no enemies. If the snake is alive, you have some.

Tipton Miller, Lubbock

If you find a coiled snake in a cow trail, you must kill it. If
you don't, that same snake will bite your horse the
next time you pass this way again.

Jewell Gilliam, Brownfield

Kill the first snake that you see in the spring and you will
have no enemies all spring.

Dean Cook, Fort Worth

A hoop snake takes his tail in his mouth and rolls away
from danger.

Keith Chamblis, Lubbock

A joint snake in times of danger breaks into joints,
rejoining himself when the danger is past.

Keith Chamblis, Lubbock

A snake track that crosses a road is a good luck sign. If the
snake has crossed the road beforehand, it is not still
around to bite you.

Lucy Basedow, San Antonio

A snake will always return to its dead mate, so if you kill
one snake, look for two.

Lewis Vicknair, Belton

If you burn a dead snake, you will never be troubled by
snakes again.

H. M Gathling, San Antonio

Don't carry a rope through the house or a snake will follow
you.

Molly Baker, Nixon

An old dog knows the shortest way to a rabbit's nest.
Robert Andrews, Gatesville

Hang a snake upside down on a barbed wire fence and
there will be a good rain.

Mrs. C. P. Davis, Lubbock

A yellow cat will go to people who hate it and will try to
make them love it by rubbing around the people's
ankles and mewing "More love, more love."

Mrs. Edna Ferguson, Salado

If a turtle bites a person, it will not let go until it thunders.
Mrs. J. T. Shahan, Bracketville

Spit on a fish hook to make the fish bite.

Olive Wheeler, Lubbock

Home and Hearth

Love, Marriage, Home and Children

If you sneeze before breakfast, you will see your true love before Saturday night.

Linda Shile, Plainview

Giving a bride-to-be or a newborn baby a silver dollar will bring the recipient good luck.

Eleanor Cossiart, San Antonio

Marry in blue, your love will be true.
Marry in brown, you will live in town.
Marry in green, you will be ashamed to be seen.
Marry in red, you will wish yourself dead.
Marry in white, you and your love will fight.
Marry in black, you will wish yourself back.
Marry in yellow, your lover will be jealous.
Marry in pink, your love will sink.

Mrs. John Davis, Matador

Say the ABC's as you twist the stem of an apple off and the letter at which the stem comes off is the first initial of your lover's name.

Maude Barker, Gilliland

If you take the last cookie on a dish, you will be an old maid.

Neven Lindsay, Kilgore

If the left thumb is on top when a man clasps his hands
together, he will rule the house; if the right thumb
is on top, his wife will rule. If a girl's second toe is
longer than her big toe, she will rule the house.
Mary Jo Henderson, Fort Worth

The first time you sleep in a room, name the four corners
boys' names. The corner you look at first when you
awake will have the name of the boy you will marry.
Tina Cooper, Pleasanton

Cold hands, warm heart;
Dirty feet, no sweetheart.
Suzanne Brown, San Antonio

If a maiden completes a patchwork quilt alone, she will
never marry.
David Hurt, Lubbock

If one looks in a well at twelve o'clock noon, one will see his
futuremate.
Maude Barker, Gilliland

Some East Texans believe that if you put an axe under the
bed it will act as a contraceptive.
Gardis Weidman, San Antonio

If a girl will sleep on a piece of wedding cake, she will dream
    of the one she will marry.

>   *Kay Lanceley, Big Spring*

If you want to find out who you are going to marry, place
    a pulley bone over the door; the first person to come
    under it will be the one.

>   *A. M. Bledsoe, Helotes*

If you stump your toe,
Kiss your thumb
And you'll see your beau.

>   *Nancy Hurt, Lubbock*

It is bad luck for a bride to cut the ribbons on a wedding gift;
    it will cut a friendship.

>   *Katherine Hepner, Big Spring*

Strike a kitchen match, hold the flame upward, let it burn
    until the charred stem curls, or curves. In whatever
    direction the curved stem points, that is the direc-
    tion in which the holder of the match must go to find
    his sweetheart.

>   *Keith Chamblis, Lubbock*

'He loves me; he loves me not.' These sentences can be said
   either while pulling the petals off a flower or by
   twisting a straw and counting the twists until the
   straw breaks. Whichever the last petal or twist
   lands on is the verdict.

Gloria Nathanson, Brownsville

Eat every grain of rice in your bowl or you will have a
   spouse who has chicken pox marks.

Lorena Sims, Lubbock

Never give a lover a pair of scissors for they will cut the love
   in two.

Mattie Green, Lubbock

If you see a red bird in the woods, you will see your
   sweetheart before night.

Joyce Sales, Lubbock

When you have finished quilting a new quilt, put a cat in
   the center of the quilt and shake it. Let single girls
   hold corners of the quilt and do the shaking. When
   the shaking ends, the girl that the cat runs by is the
   one who will get married.

Kay Lanceley, Big Spring

The sun shining on your wedding day means a good
   marriage.

Suzanne Brown, San Antonio

Only a flighty woman
Can cook candy;
It takes sense to make biscuits.
Mrs. Laura Perkins, Bartlett

If a girl gives her lover a cat, they will break up and never get back together again.
Loretta Spinner, Amarillo

Never take off a wedding ring, for that means that one of the couple will die.
Earl Turner, Clyde

If you drop two forks at the same place setting, there will be a wedding in the family.
Jane Buchanan, Lubbock

A bride will have a child for every ribbon she cuts at her showers.
Eleanor Cossiart, San Antonio

Count seven different stars for seven consecutive nights and you will dream about the person you will marry.
Keith Chamblis, Lubbock

If a mirror is held over a cistern or a well on the first day of April, the image of the true love of the person holding the mirror will appear.
Marie Miles, Lubbock

A girl can place a wet handkerchief out in the evening so
the moonlight will catch it and in the morning, the
initials of her lover will be found in the wrinkles that
the moon has made.

John Coffey, Itasca

Three times a bridesmaid, never a bride.

Wanda Cunningham, Paris

May is an unlucky month for marriage.

Mattie Green, Lubbock

The number of seeds which you find while eating an orange
will indicate the number of lovers you will have in
your life.

Lonnie Dillard, Lubbock

Don't eat watermelons if you are pregnant because your
baby will be premature if you do.

Judy Moffett, Lubbock

Tape a silver dollar on a baby's navel and the navel will go
in.

Frank Medley, Jarrell

If a pregnant woman is scared by an animal, the baby will
resemble that animal when it arrives.
Jack Lancaster, Plainview

One can predict the sex of an unborn baby by holding a
pendulum above the mother's abdomen. If the
pendulum swings east to west, the baby is a girl;
if it swings north and south, the baby is a boy.
Sharon Boatman, Lubbock

If a pregnant woman goes out of the house during the
eclipse of the sun, she will lose her child.
Maude Barker, Gilliland

Children born in March will have flighty minds.
Gardis Weidman, San Antonio

The pregnant woman must be careful where she places
her hand if she becomes excited or sees something
unsightly. She might mark the baby.
Joyce Sales, Lubbock

When old-fashioned mothers nursed their babies, they
first consulted the signs of the Zodiac in the
almanac. If the signs were in the head, it was
adjudged criminal to wean the infant then. If the
signs pointed to the heart, the baby would cry
easily all his life. But if the signs pointed to the
stomach, weaning would kill him. Therefore, the

safest time, with the least aftereffects, was when
the signs were in the legs or the feet: the signs
were leaving then.

George Wilson, Lubbock

Wean babies by the full moon.

Judith Adams, Lubbock

If a pregnant woman has chronic hiccoughs, her child
will have a great deal of hair.

Darlene Austin, Bandera

If a child's nails are cut with scissors before it is a year
old, it will grow up to be a thief.

Donna Bain, Amarillo

If a child cries on its first birthday, it will be unhappy
throughout life.

David Hurt, Lubbock

Children are warned against throwing a crust of bread
or an unwanted bit of food into the open fire.
They are told that doing so is 'feeding the devil.'

George Wilson, Lubbock

If a stranger touches a Mexican child while visiting its
home, the mother will touch the stranger for good
luck before he leaves.

Donna King, Lubbock

Let a baby under one year look in a mirror and it will
    die. (This is true, although it may take 101
    years.)
                Robert Alldredge, Floydada

If an expectant mother spends too much time with her
    hair, the baby will have a cowlick.
                Jack Miles, Gillett

Birthmarks were thought to be caused by shock or fright
    during pregnancy.
                Paul Hollerman, Austin

If you permit someone to sweep under your feet, you will
    never marry.
                Mrs. Edward Perkins, Holland

A child born with a blue ring on its nose will not live to
    wear clothes.
                Jolene Biggers, Taylor

If you make a wish when the groom-to-be puts your
    engagement ring on, the wish will hold until the
    ring is removed from the finger.
                Phillip Egger, Brownwood

Pass a new baby three times around a table leg to bring
    it good luck.
                Jenny Lowell, Georgetown

If a bride wants to be happy, she should step over the church still with her right foot.

Frances Walzek, Walburg

Shake the tablecloth out of doors after sunset and you will never marry.

Mrs. C. P. Davis, Lubbock

In every marriage, each person has a job. One makes the living, and the other one makes the living worthwhile.

H. M. Gathling, San Antonio

Never bring an axe into the house. If you forget and bring one in, always take it back out the same door through which you brought it in.

R. D. Filler, Fort Worth

A new broom sweeps clean, but an old broom knows where the dirt is.

Mrs. C. P. Davis, Lubbock

If you drop anything sharp and it sticks upright, make a wish before pulling it out, and it will come true.

Billy Joyce Whaley, Post

If a pregnant woman lifts her arms above her head, the
   umbilical cord will wrap around the baby and
   strangle it.
   Jack Lancaster, Plainview

A child born during a storm will have a happy
   disposition.
   Martha Kissinger, Fort Worth

If an unborn child is carried high in the womb, it is sure
   to be a girl; if it is carried low, it will be a boy.
   Chris Matthews, Dallas

To determine the sex of an unborn baby, note the shape
   of the mother's stomach: If the stomach is oblong
   like a football, the baby will be a girl; if the
   stomach is round like a basketball, the baby will
   be a boy.
   Lonnie Dillard, Lubbock

It is bad to have a cat in the house if you have a baby,
   because if the cat breathes in the baby's face, the
   baby will die.
   Susan Eklund, San Antonio

A pregnant woman should not smell paint, hang up
   clothes, or see an accident.
   Sue Dial, San Antonio

Clothing

If you put on your socks inside out, wear them that way
until noon. You will have good luck the rest of the
day.

Anna Bridges, San Antonio

If you put one sock on inside out, you must change it to
have it on the right way before you take a single
step; if you take a step with one sock turned
inside out, you must wear your socks that way all
day long. If you don't, you will have bad luck.

Mrs. C. P. Davis, Lubbock

Never trust a widow woman in a yellow dress.

Frances Roberts, Walburg

A widely known rodeo superstition concerns the old ten-
gallon hat. If a hat is thrown on a bed in the
presence of a cowboy who is to ride a bucking bull
that day, he will feel as if that will be his last
ride. A hat on the bed spells bad luck.

Virginia Butler, Lubbock

If someone finds the hem of your dress turned up, you
    are going to get a new one.

Tina Cooper, Pleasanton

Kiss the turned-up hem of your dress and make a wish;
    it will come true.

Mrs. Amanda Ponder, Austin

If you put on a garment wrong side out, you will have
    bad luck unless you let a left-handed person
    change it for you.

Felicia Jones, Holland

If you put something on wrong side out while you are
    getting dressed, don't take it off and put it on
    correctly. Wear it as you put it on and you will
    get a new one soon.

Eleanor Cossiart, San Antonio

Never take off and put on correctly a shirt or dress
    which has been accidentally put on wrong side
    out. To do so is to invite bad luck of the worst
    sort.

Charles Ricker, Lubbock

A new hat looks good, but the old one knows the shape
of your head.

W. D. Davis, Granger

If you wear a friend's shirt for two days, you will be
friends forever.

Charles Simpson, Fort Worth

If your best friend's cowboy boots will fit you, you and
he should exchange boots once in a while—
especially if you have been having a streak of bad
luck; to change boots will change your luck.

Howard Pearson, Matador

Never wear a previously unworn garment to a funeral.

Mrs. Laura Perkins, Bartlett

If you wear all new clothes to a wedding, the bride will
blush.

Freda Hilton, Littlefield

A girl who wears a man's clothing is sure to be wild.

Doris Henry, Menard

A person whose pants are always unpressed will usually
have a jolly disposition.

Holly Matthews, Freeport

A man in a silk shirt never picked much cotton.
W. D. Davis, Granger

If you have a hole in your pants, you will get a letter if
no one tells you about the hole.
Bessie Wilder, Alpine

If you turn a shoe upside down in the door, the owls will
quit hollering.
Maude Barker, Gilliland

Never place shoes under a bed; it is bad luck to do so.
Mildred Hoghland, Perryton

It is bad luck to place shoes on a rack higher than one's
head.
Irene McCrystal, San Antonio

You must sew all your troubles up in a pillowcase on
the first day of the year, and they won't bother
you anymore.
Elizabeth Hawkins, Lubbock

Always put your left shoe on first to guide your feet on
   the path.

Suzanne Brown, San Antonio

See a pin and pick it up
And all the day
You'll have good luck.

See a pin and let it lay
And to good luck
You say good day.

Amy Roberts, San Marcos

Health Lore

If there are onions in a house where there is sickness,
they will pick up the sick germs, so don't eat these
onions.

Anne Jenkins, Deer Park

A man whose mother died without ever having seen him
can cure a baby's colic or thrush by breathing on
the baby. (Thrush is a fungal disease of the
mouth.)

Judith Adams, Lubbock

To get rid of a sty, repeat the rhyme:

Go to the crossroads, leave my eye,
Catch the first fool that passes by.

Loretta Spinner, Lubbock

Drinking milk with fish is poisonous as is drinking milk
with chili.

William Lucero, Belton

If a child drinks coffee, he will grow a long nose.

Irene McCrystal, San Antonio

To get rid of warts, rub a piece of binder twine on the
warts, bury the twine in a damp place, and don't
tell anyone where you buried it.

Emma Beights, Lubbock

In Texas and Louisiana where malaria is prevalent and
chills are common, it is believed that if you take a
black string and tie a knot in it for every day you
have had a chill, then add an extra knot for the
current day, and hang the string in a dogwood
tree, the chills will leave you.

Sam Harmon, Beaumont

Rheumatism can be cured by carrying an Irish potato in
the pocket until it shrivels. The potato absorbs
the poison and the rheumatism leaves you. Brass
finger rings also ward off rheumatism.

Fern Ringer, Gladewater

Make a perfect remedy for rheumatism by placing thirty
pecan halves in thirty tablespoons of good bour-
bon whiskey; let the pecan halves soak in the
whiskey in a tightly closed jar for thirty days.
Then, drink a tablespoon of the whiskey twice
daily and eat one pecan half with each tablespoon
of whiskey.

Robert Ford, Bartlett

Eat a bite of garlic every morning before breakfast in
order to insure against colds and flu or grippe.
O. V. Warren, De Leon

Wash your hair with tar soap and it will make it curl.
Tilly Wagner, San Antonio

Remedy for heart failure: ten cents worth of cloves, ten
cents worth of cinnamon bark pulverized, put in
a quart of pure whiskey. Take a teaspoon three
times a day.
Billy Joyce Whaley, Post

What can't be cured
Must be endured.
Rose Mayfield, Brownfield

Eat a dish made of the leaves of the poke weed to
cleanse the body of impurities. Eat this dish in
the spring. Leaves must be parboiled, then
cooked.
Alma Taylor, Wellman

Flour, browned in the oven to a light golden color, is
good for rashes, especially baby rashes.
Gardis Weidman, San Antonio

When a little dogie has loose bowels, mix kerosene and
raw eggs together and pour it down its mouth.
Otto Lehramann, Sagerton

A good cure for dropsy is ashes and charcoal.
Paula Steele, Dallas

Tea of pumpkin seeds kills tapeworms.
John Halsey, Lubbock

A salve made of sulphur, lard, and kerosene is a sure
cure for the seven-year itch.
Ernest Sigmon, San Antonio

To treat a rusty-nail puncture wound, soak the foot in a
bucket of coal oil to stop soreness and take the
poison out.
R. D. Filler, Fort Worth

Walk around the house barefooted in the first snow of
the season and you will stay healthy all winter.
Fred Douglas, Lubbock

Calamus roots, when chewed, will cure the cramps.
Lou Williams, Jarrell

A copper wire worn about the wrist or ankle will prevent
or cure rheumatism.
Thomas Karle, Temple

To cure croup, tie a black shoestring about the patient's
    neck.

Fred Liles, Waxahachie

A good cure for croup is a teaspoon of sugar with a drop
    or two of kerosene in it.

C. H. Hamblin, Holland

For every gray hair pulled out of your head, two more
    will appear.

Alice Seewald, Boerne

If you put ink on warts, they will disappear.

Alma Taylor, Wellman

If a baby has the hives, give it mare's milk and it will
    soon be well.

Marie Cornett, Hawkins

If you steal a dishrag and hide it, your warts will disap-
    pear when the rag begins to rot.

Ruth Sheek, Pettit

If your ears burn and turn red, someone is talking about
    you and is not being complimentary.

Eleanor Cossiart, San Antonio

Take sulphur and molasses in the spring as a tonic.

Randolph Holland, Belton

If your nose bleeds, put a large, metal house key at the
nape of your neck to stop the bleeding.
Marie Miles, Lubbock

When a person has chills and is shivering, it is said that
a wolf is walking over his grave.
Claudette McInnis, May

A child who is very ill will recover if you feed it tea
made from chicken-house manure.
Irene Kuykendall, Lubbock

Wearing a small sack of garlic around one's neck will
keep illness away (and friends).
Mrs. J. W. Hilton, Borger

If a child has chickenpox, take him through a chicken
house. To do so will cure or lighten his case.
Mildred Hoghland, Perryton

Bury the cut-off parts of your hair when you get a hair-
cut and your hair will be prettier.
Mary Lackey, Lubbock

Hang asafetida around a child's neck so it will not catch
disease.
Mrs. Laura Perkins, Bartlett

Kerosene applied to snake bite will draw out the poison.
R. L. Laughringer, Floresville

Rubbing a wart and repeating magic words will cause
the wart to disappear. Sometimes, only seventh
daughters of seventh daughters know the right
magic words.

Mrs. Neven Linsay, Kilgore

Spinach will put hair on your teeth.

Irene McCrystal, San Antonio

To cure warts permanently, just before sunup go out and
find an old bone. Face the sun and rub the old
bone over the warts. Then throw the old bone
over your right shoulder and never look back.

Sharon Boatman, Lubbock

A chew of tobacco (already chewed) bound over a scor-
pion sting brings instant relief.

Mrs. Joe Moore, Post

To avoid poison ivy allergy, eat three leaves of the plant
in the early spring.

Mildred Balwin, San Antonio

Prickly pear pads with the spines burned away applied
to the joints will relieve the pain of rheumatism.

Elida Sepulveda, San Antonio

To bring a boil to a head, use a prickly pear poultice.
Molly Baker, Nixon

To cure rabies or snakebite, place a moonstone on the
animal bitten.
Jack Miles, Gillett

A way to get rid of warts is to pick the wart, let some
blood from it drop on a grain of corn, and feed the
grain to a chicken.
Virginia Adams, Lubbock

Put bacon on a boil to draw the poison out.
Mildred Adams, Gatesville

An old remedy for people with a 'nervous condition' is to
walk barefooted over newly planted ground.
Mrs. Ennis Miller, Belton

Eating onions helps cure colds.
Beverly Harris, Odessa

If a baby drinks water from a shoe of someone who had
not seen his father, the baby will be cured of
hives.
Mrs. Eunice Johnson, Plainview

For dysentery, one may chew live oak buds.
Bob Sparks, Alice

Boil poke sallet root and then use the water to bathe in.
    If this is done seven days in a row, it will cure the
    itch.
Mrs. John Davis, Matador

For a boil, crush the leaves of jimpson weed and apply to
    the sore area. This will draw it to a head.
Joe Moore, Post

Mexican cure for pin worms: Grind and eat mesquite
    beans. If this doesn't kill you, it will surely cure
    you.
Mrs. Phil Koonce, Pleasanton

To cure asthma, back the victim up to a tree and drive a
    nail into the tree two inches above the head.
    When the victim grows to this mark, his asthma
    will disappear.
Willie Salinas, Post

A cure for dysentery is to make tea from the white part
    inside the bark of the mesquite and drink it.
Hicks Turner, San Antonio

To cure rheumatism, tie a dime in a handkerchief and
    wear it around your knee.
William Gary, Canyon

To ease the pain of a sprained ankle, wrap it in brown
    paper soaked in vinegar.
                                    R. D. Filler, Fort Worth

Carry a buckeye in your right hip pocket to cure rheu-
    matism.
                                    Claude Davis, Lubbock

If you eat parched egg shells, it will keep you from wet-
    ting the bed.
                                    John Whitman, Menard

Eating the neck of a chicken is supposed to make you
    beautiful.
                                    Anne Whitmeyer, Midland

If you sleep with your head to the west, you will wake
    up with a headache.
                                    Margo Reed, Lubbock

If you have to sneeze and can't, look at the sun.
                                    Frank Ramsey, Lubbock

If your nose is bleeding, put a dime in your mouth be-
    tween your jaw teeth and press down on it; this
    will stop the bleeding.
                                    Susan Bower, Port Arthur

If you look a person who has sore eyes straight in the
eye, you will catch them, too.

B. F. Kellum, Lubbock

Wear a cotton string around your ankle, and you will
not have leg cramps.

Mrs. George Hood, Lipan

To remove warts, bury the same number of beans as you
have warts. As you walk off, do not look back.
Your warts will leave in one day.

Alva Holman, Lubbock

To cure T.B., sleep near a goat pen.

Elizabeth Hawkins, Lubbock

To cure hay-fever, get stung by eight or nine bees.

Paula Steele, Lubbock

To cure warts, tie a knot in a string for each wart you
have. Hide the string and don't tell anyone where
it is and never go back to the place where you put
the string.

Thad Allison, Richardson

Ears, Eyes, and Other Body Parts

A boil in the nose signifies that you will 'smell' a
    wedding.
                    Juanita Reasonover, Wellman

If your ear itches, you will hear a secret.
                    Eugenia McNeill, Crosbyton

If one of your ears burns, someone is talking about you:
    left ear, it's bad; right ear, it's good.
                    Suzanne Brown, San Antonio

If your nose itches,
Along will come a man
With a hole in his britches.
                    Evelyn Pursch, Pleasanton

If your ears ring, someone is walking over your grave.
                    Kay Lanceley, Big Spring

If someone notices that you have an eyelash loose, she
    should tell you and you should make a wish.
    Then, if you can guess which eye the loose lash
    is on, your wish will come true.
                    Tina Cooper, Pleasanton

Itching palms concern money: left palm—you will spend
money; right palm—you'll receive it.

Suzanne Brown, San Antonio

If your right hand itches, you will get a letter which
pleases you; if your left hand itches, you will get a
letter which displeases you.

Martha Brown, Lubbock

If your lip itches, you are going to kiss someone.

Ann Banks, Lubbock

If your right foot itches, you are going to walk on a new
location.

Jim McGraw, Amarillo

If your left hand itches, you will shake hands with a
stranger.

Claude Davis, Lubbock

When you bite your tongue, it is a sign you told a lie.

Bess Cooper, Holland

Ingrown toenails mean a stingy disposition. To cure
ingrown toenails, cut them straight across with a
pair of silver scissors on the decrease of the moon.
By the time there is a new moon, the nails will
have grown out.

Georgia Price, Taylor

If you bite your fingernails, you will have worms.
Betty Jackson, Bartlett

A bald-headed man never has cancer.
John Jones, Ozona

If you have a cowlick on the crown of your head, you will
eat bread in two kingdoms.
Mrs. Laura Perkins, Bartlett

A man who is knock-kneed can be trusted with the
management of property.
T. B. Lewis, Holland

If your eyebrows curl downward, you will travel to three
continents before you die.
Jerry Hughes, Salado

Beware a tall woman who is splayfooted; she is the
bringer of bad news and will tell lies on you.
John Lott, Waco

If you twist your ankle (sprain it) twice in a week's time,
you will get new boots.
William Landman, Fort Stockton

A man with little or no hair on his chest will be a poet or
a visionary and will never go bald.
Cindy Plume, Victoria

If you pull an eyelash, place it between your thumb and
forefinger, make a wish, and guess whether it will
stick to the thumb or finger. If you open your
hand and find that you guessed right, your wish
will come true.

Lonnie Dillard, Lubbock

If a tooth comes out and you don't put your tongue into
the tooth hole until a new tooth has grown in, the
new tooth will be gold.

Rowena Williams, Lubbock

If you have a bump on your tongue, you have told a fib.

G. N. Wynn, Lubbock

A dimple in chin
The devil is within.

Alma Taylor, Wellman

If your nose itches, it means that company will come.

Jane Buchanan, Lubbock

If your right eye itches, do not scratch it, but have someone else whose eyes do not itch scratch his left eye
(and vice versa) and that will soothe your eye.

Keith Chamblis, Lubbock

A woman with fuzzy cheeks will never marry a stranger.
Bessie Skinner, Davilla

If you cannot see light between your fingers when you
press them closely together and hold the hand up
to the sun, you will hold on to money well.
Freida Strong, Conroe

If your nose itches, you are going to kiss a fool.
Susan Taylor, Dallas

A man who has one blue eye and one brown one can see
into the future and can read your mind, so be
careful what you think when you see him coming
down the road.
Harold Clemmons, Troy

If your big toe is the longest one of your toes, you will
walk on strange shores before you are fifty years
old.
Andrew Barrier, Brownsville

If you weigh at fifty what you weighed at twenty-five,
you will live to be a hundred.
James Wilson, Lampasas

It is bad luck to comb your hair after dark.
Pat Guess, Bay City

A woman whose body is pear-shaped can predict the sex
of an unborn baby and tell if a pregnant woman
will have twins.

Randal Ponder, Corpus Christi

If you sew a dress on a Sunday, when you get to Heaven
you will have to take every stitch out with your
nose.

Mrs. Helen Braun, Lubbock

Long hair should never burn the combings; to do so will
cause the hair to come out or fall. Hair combings
must be rolled in neat balls and thrown in the
yard for the birds to nest with.

George Williams, Dumas

The best toothbrush is made by chewing the end of a
small mesquite twig until it can be shaped as a
brush. Then brush your teeth with soda or with
vinegar and salt.

Mrs. A. Vick, Caddo

White flecks under your fingernails are signs you have
told lies.

Jim Cooper, Holland

If your right palm itches, you'll shake hands with a
    stranger.

Gladys Cage, San Antonio

If your left palm itches, you are going to get some
    money.

John H. Cage, San Antonio

If your foot itches, it's a sign you are going to a new
    place.

Martha Brown, Lubbock

Departing This World, Or Heaven Can't Wait

The last words of a dying person should be considered
words of pure wisdom; they can also give a
glimpse of heaven.

Suzanne Brown, San Antonio

If a member of the family dies and his corpse is in the
house, cover all mirrors with some sort of drapery
until the body has been removed and buried;
otherwise, the first member of the family to see
himself in the mirror will die before the year is
out.

Eugenia Reiwald, San Antonio

Whistling at the table,
Singing in bed,
The devil will get you
Before you are dead.

Loretta Spinner, Lubbock

A rooster crowing at the back door signifies the death of
some member of the family.

Mrs. C. P. Davis, Lubbock

When a lone buzzard is circling high overhead, it is said
that someone near the person who sees the buzzard is going to die. A rhyme is sometimes said
when a lone buzzard is seen: "Pallbearer, pallbearer in the sky, tell me today who will die."
Claudette McInnis, May

If you have the jitters, accompanied by chills running up
and down your spine, it means that a rabbit is
running over the site of your grave.
Patsy Smith, San Antonio

If a bird flies in through an open window, it is a sign of a
coming death in the family.
Judith Adams, Lubbock

Two knives placed beside a plate means death.
Frances Williams, Holland

If a branch dies on a willow tree, someone in the family
will die.
Norma Thomas, Lubbock

Death comes by threes or by sevens. (If there is one
death in a family or neighborhood, there will soon
be two or six more.)
Anna Kirk, Lubbock

When a hen crows, it means death in the family.
Maude Barker, Gilliland

If a dog howls at midnight, someone will die that same
night.

Marshall Hayes, Lott

If a moth flutters in your face while you are tending a
sick person, it's a sure sign of death.

Pat Guess, Bay City

A screech owl at night means a death in the family. If
you hear one, tie a knot in a handkerchief to
make him stop and to break the spell.

Mrs. A. Vick, Caddo

Hearing a dove coo three times near one's home means
that there will be a death in the family in the
near future.

Mrs. Max Schaefer, San Antonio

If you sneeze three times on Sunday morning before
breakfast, you will hear of a death that will affect
you personally.

Marie Cornett, Lubbock

If you see a white dove light upon the ground, you will
get a death message.

Thelma Stuart, Lubbock

It is bad luck to walk over a grave.

Doris Di Quinzio, Hondo

If an owl hoots at night, take a broom and put it in the
hallway to stop a death in the family.

Mrs. Ennis Miller, Belton

If a kerosene lamp goes out when there is still oil in its
tank, it is a sure sign of a death in the family.

Anne Bridges, San Antonio

If the same picture falls off the wall three times someone is going to die.

Milton Thornton, Lubbock

If you plant a willow tree and it makes a shade, you will
die.

Ann Banks, Lubbock

Don't watch someone out of sight or you won't see them
alive again.

Mrs. C. P. Davis, Lubbock

If one person dies in the community, there will be two in
succession.

Velma Parker, Temple

It is bad luck if it rains in an open grave, for another
member of the family will die before the year is
out.

Tipton Miller, Thorndale

Do not plant a cedar tree on a grave. When the cedar
covers the grave, a member of the family will die.

Darleen Stevens, Lubbock

Hold your breath and cross your fingers when a graveyard is passed.

Jane Buchanan, Lubbock

If you plant evergreens, you will die when they are tall
enough to cover the length of your grave.

Mrs. W. R. Crownover, Big Spring

It is bad luck to count cars in a funeral procession.

Hazel Dahnke, Lubbock

If you see a dog shudder three times in his sleep, you
will soon have a death message.

John Jones, Ozona

Blessed are the dead the rain falls on.

Donny Kelsey, Killeen

If a water dog (salamander) barks at you, you will die.

B. F. Kellum, Lubbock

Hold your breath when you pass a graveyard and you
will live a long life.

Tom Weatherford, Bartlett

There is a death pending when the whippoorwill cries
near your house.

Sara Brown, Floresville

If you see an ambulance or hearse, you should take hold
of a button on your shirt or dress or you will be
the next person to ride in the ambulance or
hearse.

Evelyn Berry, Temple

The name of a certain constellation to be seen in the
winter sky is 'Job's Coffin.' This constellation is
in the shape of an oldtime coffin.

Betty Bennett, Waco

If any tool that could be used for digging a grave is
brought into the house, some member of that
household will die.

Patrick Jobe, Victoria

To avoid sorrow when you see a lone buzzard in the sky,
stand and watch until the buzzard flaps out of
sight.

Maxine Fuller, Salado

Don't rock a chair with no one in it or someone will die.

Mattie Green, Lubbock

Make a wish when going by a graveyard. Be sure to
    cross your fingers, shut your eyes, and bite your
    tongue as you make the wish.
                            Gladys Johnson, Holland

Never talk while you are passing a cemetery or you will
    surely have bad luck.
                            Curtis Pearce, Rockdale

In the days of kerosene lamps, if the chimney began to
    smoke, a ghost was prowling the room.
                            George Wilson, Lubbock

If you are out horseback riding on a summer's night and
    pass through a patch of warm air, you have been
    in the company of 'hain'ts' (ghosts or spirits).
                            Jim Cooper, Holland

When your candles burn low and blue, there is a ghost
    in the room.
                            Bud Garner, Taylor

Superstitions

A Grab Bag of Superstitions

Give a knife as a present, but make sure the giver pays
you a penny or your friendship will be cut in two.
Anne Banks, Lubbock

To tell if a cow is with calf, put a silver dollar to its
navel and the calf will kick.
Earl Plemmons, Val Verde

Tie a red rag around the trunk of a fruit tree to keep the
eclipse of the sun from knocking the fruit off.
Maude Barker, Gilliland

If you drop a fork, a woman is coming.
If you drop a knife, a man is coming.
If you drop a spoon, a child is coming.
Mrs. Roy Craig, Stamford

If a farmer finds a bad potato, he should throw it over
the nearest building to guarantee a good crop.
Brenda Vernon, Georgetown

It is bad luck to give anyone a purse or a billfold without just a little money in it.
Mary Francis Adair, Houston

When eating the pulleybone of a chicken, two people can
use it to wish on. Two people pull it apart, and
the one that gets the longest half will get married
first, and the one with the short half will get his
wish.

Jane Buchanan, Lubbock

As full of superstition
As an egg is of chicken.

Rose Mayfield, Brownfield

Cowboys hate to bypass a beggar for fear that their
stinginess will bring bad luck.

Virginia Butler, Austin

If your eyesight is growing weak, grow a mustache. The
longer the mustache becomes, the better you can
see.

Peggy Carter, Ralls

It is bad luck for a woman to go out to the rig when it is
time for the oil well to come in.

Helen Carwile, Kermit

It is bad luck to walk across a porch with a hoe.

Mrs. C. P. Davis, Lubbock

If a child plays in the fire, he will wet the bed at night.
Keith Chamblis, Lubbock

If you have served yourself at the table and without re-
alizing it, placed a second serving on the plate,
you can be sure that hungry people are coming.
Tina Cooper, Pleasanton

To find oil or water, drill on a hill-top, never in a valley.
Marie Cornett, Lubbock

To see if a watermelon is ripe without plugging it, bal-
ance a straw crosswise on the watermelon. If it is
ripe, the straw will pivot parallel to the length of
the melon.
Lonnie Dillard, Lubbock

If you run until you have a stitch in your side, bend
over, pick up a rock, and spit under it.
Pat Guess, Bay City

A person whose eyebrows grow together across his fore-
head will be rich some day; such a person is also
very jealous natured.
Mrs. W. L. Campbell, Fort Worth

There is always oil under a graveyard.
Tom Weatherford, Bartlett

When you drop your comb, step on it before you pick it
up. This will ward off the evil spirits.

Barbara Holloway, Dallas

If a person hands you an open knife, hand it back to him
open; if he hands it to you closed, hand it back to
him closed.

Sammie Miller, Brownfield

If a spider drops down in front of you, you will receive a
letter.

T. L. Miller, Lubbock

After framing a quilt, you must quilt a few stitches on it
the same day or you will never get it finished.

Juanita Reasonover, Wellman

Carrying a buckeye in your pocket means good luck for
sure.

Laverne Salyer, San Antonio

You can start going barefooted in the spring when you
see the first scissortail.

Tulisha Shahan, Bracketville

If a person wants to say something but cannot remem-
ber it, it is a lie.

Loretta Spinner, Lubbock

If you kiss your elbow, you will change your sex.

Rowena Williams, Lubbock

What you do on New Year's Day, you will be doing all year.

Dorothy Ponder, Elgin

When you find money (a coin), never spend it or give it away. Keep it, and you will continue to find more. If you spend it, you will break your luck.

Eleanor Cossiart, San Antonio

The burning of red onion peels will bring good luck.

Mary Aven, San Antonio

If there is a feather in your hair when you awake in the morning, this means that you are going to travel.

Mrs. Howard French, Spur

If you break your washpot, you will have twenty years bad luck.

Mrs. Roy Craig, Stamford

Opals bring bad luck.

Irene McCrystal, San Antonio

A new penny brings good luck.

Kay Thornton, Lubbock

Bringing a hoe in the house is bad luck.
Grace Davis, Granger

Go out the same door of the house that you used to enter
the house. To do so will bring good luck.
Sarah Harris, Round Rock

After a house is built and the family moves into it, it is
bad luck to cut another window for the house.
Mattie Green, Lubbock

When a new home is built, the first fire to be made in
the fireplace should come from a happy and pros-
perous home to bring good luck to the new home.
Mrs. Jack Miles, Gillett

If you take an axe or hoe into a house, you must take it
out the same door you brought it in to avoid bad
luck.
Mrs. B. C. Baker, Nixon

To move a broom to a new house is bad luck unless you
throw it over the house.
Molly Baker, Nixon

If you break a mirror, bury it so that you won't have bad
luck.
Deane Smith, Bryan

If you sing early in the morning, the buzzards will pick
    the meat off your bones before night.
Mrs. Jack French, Levelland

If a horseshoe is nailed with the opening placed down-
    ward, your luck will run out.
Mrs. H. M. Gathling, San Antonio

If you find a horseshoe, spit on it, throw it over your left
    shoulder, and without looking back to where it
    fell, walk away and you will have seven years
    good luck.
Robert L. Ferguson, Clyde

A butterfly in the house means a lady will visit you
    wearing a dress the same color as the butterfly.
Robert Alldredge, Floydada

To sweep under a sick person's bed will cause him to die.
Milly Balwin, San Antonio

Never sweep dirt out the door after sundown; this is
    inviting the dead to be your guest.
George Wilson, Lubbock

To step over a broom handle is bad luck.
Hazel Dahnke, Lubbock

Never return borrowed salt. It is bad luck to do so.
Jane Buchanan, Lubbock

If you spill salt, you must throw it over your left shoulder with your right hand, or you will have bad luck.
Lonnie Dillard, Lubbock

If you are going to move into a new house, burn salt in it and it will keep the witches away.
Sunny McGinnis, Lubbock

If you forget something and have to go back in the house, sit down and raise both feet off the floor before going back out or you will have bad luck.
Ann Banks, Lubbock

If you forget something and have to go back in the house, sit down and count to ten or you will have bad luck.
Ann Banks, Lubbock

If a windowpane falls out of a window and breaks, it is a sign of death.
Mildred Hoghland, Perryton

Wherever lightning strikes, you will find oil.
Marie Cornett, Lubbock

If you sing before breakfast, you will cry before supper.
Diane Howe, San Antonio

It is bad luck to spin a chair around on one leg.
Jack Lancaster, Amarillo

If you find a penny, pick it up and put it in your left shoe
for good luck.
Mrs. Ennis Miller, Belton

It is bad luck to burn the wood of a tree that has been
struck by lightning.
Mrs. Nola James, San Angelo

When you sing after you go to bed, you will wake up
crying.
Mrs. Erma Taggart, Mount Pleasant

If two people accidentally bump heads, they will be in
the same position a year hence.
Vada Spence, Lubbock

To cut out a dress on Friday and not finish it brings bad
luck.
Maude Barker, Gilliland

If your luck is bad in gambling, strike a match and circle
the area around your head three times and you
will burn away the evil spirits.
Selma Apelman, San Antonio

Although it used to be bad luck always to move a broom,
in later years people found that you could tie out
bad luck by tying a string around the broom.
Tina Cooper, Pleasanton

If you see something dead, spit on it and say: "Not on my
mother's supper table."
Eugenia McNeill, Crosbyton